I STILL HATE CATS

SKIP MORROW

Skip Morrow

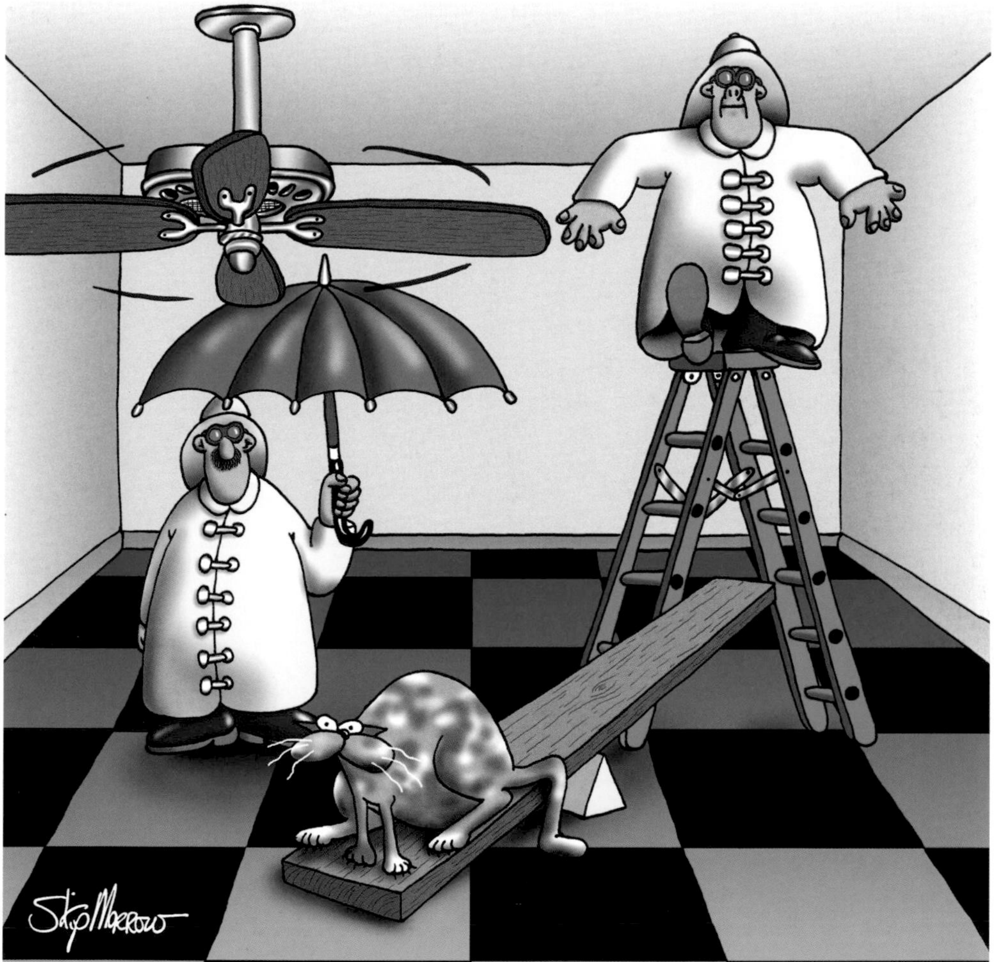
Skip Morrow

Skip Morrow

Skip Morrow

Skip Morrow

Skip Morrow

7
Skip Morrow

Skip Morrow

3 - 1 = 2
Skip Morrow

Skip Morrow

Skip Morrow

Skip Morrow

Skip Morrow

Skip Morrow

Skip Morrow

Skip Morrow

Skip Morrow

Skip Morrow

Skip Morrow

Skip Morrow

Skip Morrow

Skip Morrow

Skip Morrow

Skip Morrow

Skip Morrow

312019
Skip Morrow

Skip Morrow

Skip Morrow

Skip Morrow

Skip Morrow

SkipMorrow

Skip Morrow

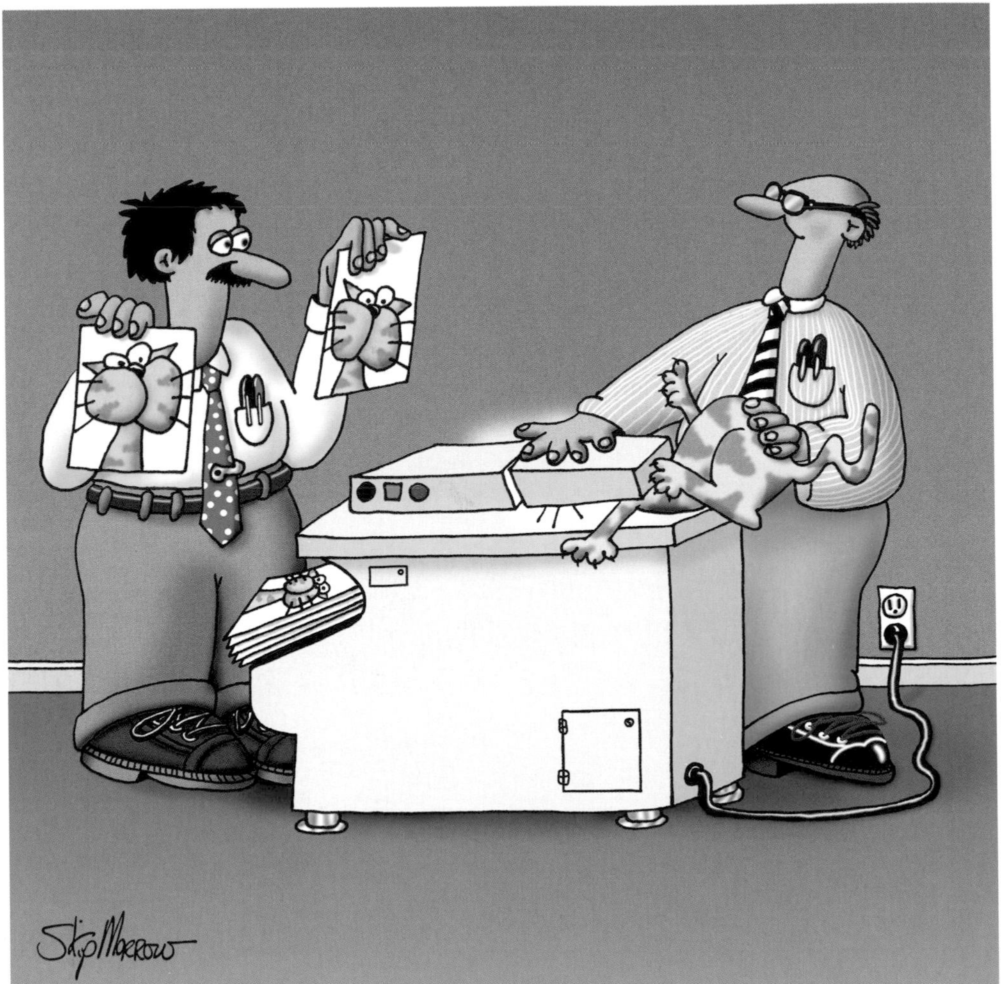

Skip Morrow

Skip Morrow

Skip Morrow

Skip Morrow

Skip Morrow

Skip Morrow

Skip Morrow

1 2 3
4 5 6
7 8 9
Skip Morrow

Skip Morrow

Skip Morrow

Skip Morrow